30
Powerful
REVELATIONS
To learn from
THE QURAN

Copyright © 2022 GoodHearted Books Inc. (info@goodheartedbooks.com)

ISBN: 978-1-988779-56-0

Dépôt légal : bibliothèque et archives nationales du Québec, 2022.
Dépôt légal : bibliothèque et archives Canada, 2022.

Created by	: Bachar Karroum
Graphic Designer	: Samuel Gabriel
Cover Designer	: Creative Hands
Content revision	: Safa Said, Mohamed Ali
Proofreader	: Amina Ahmed
Quran english version	: The Clear Quran (Dr. Khattab), Clear Quran (Talal Itani)

In the Name of God

We are once again very grateful to be able to build on our series of books to share the essence of Islam with children. This latest creation has been crafted to shine a light on the mighty wisdom of the Quran.

Through these pages, your child will be exposed to powerful revelations that were sent to the Prophet (PBUH) and will have a framework to apply these learnings in their day-to-day lives. It is our wish that these additional pages will allow your little one to further embrace their faith, connect with Allah through Dua, and absorb essential moral values that promote lifelong personal growth.

We hope that you and your little family members will enjoy this learning experience and that it will contribute to helping your children become the best version of themselves while spreading the powerful values of our beloved religion.

Glossary

♡ Allah   Arabic word for God
♡ Al-Hamdoullillah   Praise be to God
♡ Bismillah   In the Name of God
♡ Dua   Asking Allah for blessings upon yourself and others
♡ PBUH   Peace be upon him
♡ Salam   Peace

حَسْبُنَا اللَّهُ وَنِعْمَ الْوَكِيلُ

Allah is enough for us; He is the Excellent Protector

📖 WHAT THE HOLY QURAN TELLS US ABOUT THIS

(173) Those to whom the people have said, "The people have mobilized against you, so fear them." But this only increased them in faith, and they said, "Allah is enough for us; He is the Excellent Protector."

Ali 'Imran (Family of Imran) 3.173 Revealed in Madinah

الَّذِينَ قَالَ لَهُمُ النَّاسُ إِنَّ النَّاسَ قَدْ جَمَعُوا لَكُمْ فَاخْشَوْهُمْ فَزَادَهُمْ إِيمَانًا وَقَالُوا حَسْبُنَا اللَّهُ وَنِعْمَ الْوَكِيلُ ﴿١٧٣﴾

🕊 DAY # 01 🕊

☺ I CAN LEARN FROM THE QURAN

When we feel that no one is on our side, we should remember that Allah is always with us. He alone is enough.

☆ TO BECOME A BETTER PERSON

Remembering that Allah is always with me reinforces my faith. It helps me to remember that I can accomplish anything.

♡ WITH THE HELP OF ALLAH

O, Allah! Help me to remember that You are always by my side.

END WITH AL-HAMDOULLILLAH 🌙

 DAY # 01

START WITH BISMILLAH

فَإِنَّ مَعَ الْعُسْرِ يُسْرًا

With hardship comes ease

📖 WHAT THE HOLY QURAN TELLS US ABOUT THIS

(1) Did We not soothe your heart? (2) And lift from you your burden. (3) Which weighed down your back? (4) And raised for you your reputation? (5) With hardship comes ease. (6) With hardship comes ease. (7) When your work is done, turn to devotion. (8) And to your Lord turn for everything.

Ash-Sharh (The Relief) 94.6 Revealed in Makkah

أَلَمْ نَشْرَحْ لَكَ صَدْرَكَ ① وَوَضَعْنَا عَنْكَ وِزْرَكَ ② الَّذِى أَنْقَضَ ظَهْرَكَ ③ وَرَفَعْنَا لَكَ ذِكْرَكَ ④ فَإِنَّ مَعَ الْعُسْرِ يُسْرًا ⑤ إِنَّ مَعَ الْعُسْرِ يُسْرًا ⑥ فَإِذَا فَرَغْتَ فَانْصَبْ ⑦ وَإِلَى رَبِّكَ فَارْغَبْ ⑧

🕊 **DAY # 02** 🕊

☺ I CAN LEARN FROM THE QURAN

Every difficulty has its relief. The hardships we are going through at one moment won't last forever. When things get hard, we should remember that the light always follows.

☆ TO BECOME A BETTER PERSON

Knowing that every difficulty has its relief helps me to build my endurance. It helps me to learn and gain experience from any situation.

♡ WITH THE HELP OF ALLAH

O, Allah! Help me to focus on the light, on the lesson or learning from any difficult situation.

END WITH AL-HAMDOULLILLAH ☽

 DAY # 02

START WITH BISMILLAH

لَنْ يُصِيبَنَا إِلَّا مَا كَتَبَ اللَّهُ لَنَا

Nothing will ever befall us except what Allah has destined for us

 WHAT THE HOLY QURAN TELLS US ABOUT THIS

(51) Say, "Nothing will ever befall us except what Allah has destined for us. He is our Protector." So in Allah let the believers put their trust.

At-Tawbah (The Repentance) 9.51 Revealed in Madinah

قُل لَّن يُصِيبَنَا إِلَّا مَا كَتَبَ اللَّهُ لَنَا هُوَ مَوْلَانَا ۚ وَعَلَى اللَّهِ فَلْيَتَوَكَّلِ الْمُؤْمِنُونَ ﴿٥١﴾

 **DAY # 03**

☺ I CAN LEARN FROM THE QURAN

What Allah has destined for us, whether it is hardship or ease, is for our own benefit.

☆ TO BECOME A BETTER PERSON

There is something for me to learn from every experience that I live, whether good or bad. Remembering this allows me to build my tenacity and reinforce my resilience.

♡ WITH THE HELP OF ALLAH

O, Allah! Give me the energy to walk through any situation with confidence.

END WITH AL-HAMDOULLILLAH 🌙

 DAY # 03

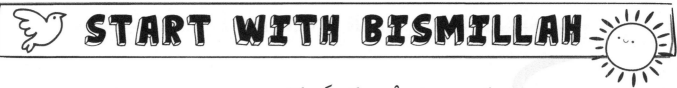

START WITH BISMILLAH

فَمَنْ يَعْمَلْ مِثْقَالَ ذَرَّةٍ خَيْرًا يَرَهُ

Whoever has done an atom's weight of good will see it

(7) Whoever has done an atom's weight of good will see it.

(8) And whoever has done an atom's weight of evil will see it.

Az-Zalzalah (The Earthquake) 99.7 Revealed in Madinah

فَمَنْ يَعْمَلْ مِثْقَالَ ذَرَّةٍ خَيْرًا يَرَهُ ۝

وَمَنْ يَعْمَلْ مِثْقَالَ ذَرَّةٍ شَرًّا يَرَهُ ۝

DAY # 04

😊 I CAN LEARN FROM THE QURAN

We should never underestimate the power of goodness. Every ounce of good that we do is rewarded. Even the smallest of good deeds.

⭐ TO BECOME A BETTER PERSON

Doing good and helping others makes my heart happy. I contribute to creating a positive environment and building great relationships.

♡ WITH THE HELP OF ALLAH

O, Allah! Help me to always do good. Please accept my good deeds.

END WITH AL-HAMDOULLILLAH 🌙

 DAY # 04

START WITH BISMILLAH

لَا يُكَلِّفُ اللَّهُ نَفْسًا إِلَّا وُسْعَهَا

Allah does not burden any soul beyond its capacity

📖 WHAT THE HOLY QURAN TELLS US ABOUT THIS

(286) Allah does not burden any soul beyond its capacity. To its credit is what it earns, and against it is what it commits. "Our Lord, do not condemn us if we forget or make a mistake (...)."

Al-Baqarah (The Cow) 2.286 Revealed in Madinah

لَا يُكَلِّفُ اللَّهُ نَفْسًا إِلَّا وُسْعَهَا ۚ لَهَا مَا كَسَبَتْ وَعَلَيْهَا مَا اكْتَسَبَتْ ۗ رَبَّنَا لَا تُؤَاخِذْنَا إِن نَسِينَا أَوْ أَخْطَأْنَا (...) ﴿٢٨٦﴾

DAY # 05

☺ I CAN LEARN FROM THE QURAN

Allah is merciful. All that He has requested from us, such as prayers, fasting, etc., are not beyond our strength. For example, if we cannot stand while praying, we can do so while sitting. Allah does not burden any soul beyond its capacity.

☆ TO BECOME A BETTER PERSON

Knowing that Allah doesn't burden me beyond my capacity helps me to reinforce my willpower. It allows me to remember that I can achieve anything through persistence.

♡ WITH THE HELP OF ALLAH

O, Allah! Give me the strength to persevere.

END WITH AL-HAMDOULLILLAH 🌙

 DAY # 05

وَأَمَّا السَّائِلَ فَلَا تَنْهَرْ

Do not rebuff the seeker

📖 WHAT THE HOLY QURAN TELLS US ABOUT THIS

(6) Did He not find you orphaned, and sheltered you? (7) And found you wandering, and guided you? (8) And found you in need, and enriched you? (9) Therefore, do not mistreat the orphan. (10) Nor rebuff the seeker. (11) But proclaim the blessings of your Lord.

Ad-Duhaa (The Morning Hours) 93.10 Revealed in Makkah

أَلَمْ يَجِدْكَ يَتِيمًا فَآوَىٰ ۝ وَوَجَدَكَ ضَالًّا فَهَدَىٰ ۝ وَوَجَدَكَ عَائِلًا فَأَغْنَىٰ ۝ فَأَمَّا الْيَتِيمَ فَلَا تَقْهَرْ ۝ وَأَمَّا السَّائِلَ فَلَا تَنْهَرْ ۝ وَأَمَّا بِنِعْمَةِ رَبِّكَ فَحَدِّثْ ۝

🕊 **DAY # 06** 🕊

☺ I CAN LEARN FROM THE QURAN

We should always open our hearts to those in need or who are asking for our help. If we have nothing to give, we should at least treat them with kindness. Allah loves those who welcome the seeker.

☆ TO BECOME A BETTER PERSON

Keeping my heart open to others makes me feel generous. Helping others reinforces my kindness and develops my empathy and compassion.

♡ WITH THE HELP OF ALLAH

O, Allah! Let me keep my heart open to others, and help those who need my help.

END WITH AL-HAMDOULLILLAH 🌙

 DAY # 06

START WITH BISMILLAH

لَئِنْ شَكَرْتُمْ لَأَزِيدَنَّكُمْ

If you are grateful, I will certainly give you more

📖 WHAT THE HOLY QURAN TELLS US ABOUT THIS

(7) And 'remember' when your Lord proclaimed, 'If you are grateful, I will certainly give you more (...).'"

Ibrahim (Ibrahim) 14.7 Revealed in Makkah

وَإِذْ تَأَذَّنَ رَبُّكُمْ لَئِنْ شَكَرْتُمْ لَأَزِيدَنَّكُمْ (٧) (...)

DAY # 07

I CAN LEARN FROM THE QURAN

When we are grateful, and we thank Allah for all that we have, we receive more blessings.

TO BECOME A BETTER PERSON

Being grateful keeps my heart full of love and free from any worry.

WITH THE HELP OF ALLAH

O, Allah! Help me to always acknowledge the good that we have and to remain grateful.

END WITH AL-HAMDOULLILLAH

DAY # 07

START WITH BISMILLAH

فَلَا تَقُل لَّهُمَآ أُفٍّ وَلَا تَنْهَرْهُمَا

Do not say to your parents a word of disrespect

📖 WHAT THE HOLY QURAN TELLS US ABOUT THIS

(23) Your Lord has commanded that you worship none but Him, and that you be good to your parents. If either of them or both of them reach old age with you, do not say to them a word of disrespect, nor scold them, but say to them kind words.

Al-Israa (The Night Journey) 17.23 Revealed in Makkah

وَقَضَىٰ رَبُّكَ أَلَّا تَعْبُدُوا إِلَّا إِيَّاهُ وَبِالْوَالِدَيْنِ إِحْسَانًا إِمَّا يَبْلُغَنَّ عِنْدَكَ الْكِبَرَ أَحَدُهُمَا أَوْ كِلَاهُمَا فَلَا تَقُل لَّهُمَا أُفٍّ وَلَا تَنْهَرْهُمَا وَقُل لَّهُمَا قَوْلًا كَرِيمًا ﴿٢٣﴾

DAY # 08

☺ I CAN LEARN FROM THE QURAN

The presence of our parents is a blessing. Allah asks that we always show them respect and be kind to them in every circumstance. We should not be rude, and we should not insult them.

☆ TO BECOME A BETTER PERSON

Being supportive and kind to my parents, in all circumstances, demonstrates my love and respect for them. Being considerate and caring towards them nourishes my soul.

♡ WITH THE HELP OF ALLAH

O, Allah! Help me to always honor my parents.

END WITH AL-HAMDOULLILLAH 🌙

 DAY # 08

START WITH BISMILLAH

وَعَسَىٰ أَنْ تَكْرَهُوا شَيْئًا وَهُوَ خَيْرٌ لَكُمْ

Perhaps you dislike something which is good for you

📖 WHAT THE HOLY QURAN TELLS US ABOUT THIS

(216) (...) Perhaps you dislike something which is good for you and like something which is bad for you. Allah knows and you do not know.

Al-Baqarah (The Cow) 2.216 Revealed in Madinah

(...) وَعَسَىٰ أَنْ تَكْرَهُوا شَيْئًا وَهُوَ خَيْرٌ لَكُمْ ۖ وَعَسَىٰ أَنْ تُحِبُّوا شَيْئًا وَهُوَ شَرٌّ لَكُمْ ۗ وَاللَّهُ يَعْلَمُ وَأَنْتُمْ لَا تَعْلَمُونَ ﴿٢١٦﴾

 **DAY # 09**

☺ I CAN LEARN FROM THE QURAN

Sometimes, when we're facing an uncomfortable situation, we may think that it's not good for us! However, even if it feels negative, this experience can lead to positive results. Allah knows what we don't know.

☆ TO BECOME A BETTER PERSON

When I don't let a negative experience affect me and place my faith in Allah, I remove all my worries. My heart remains at peace.

♡ WITH THE HELP OF ALLAH

O, Allah! Please remove my worries as I face any struggle.

END WITH AL-HAMDOULLILLAH ☽

 DAY # 09

START WITH BISMILLAH

إِنَّ بَعْضَ الظَّنِّ إِثْم

Some suspicion is sinful

📖 WHAT THE HOLY QURAN TELLS US ABOUT THIS

(12) O you who believe! Avoid most suspicion—some suspicion is sinful. And do not spy on one another, nor backbite one another (...)

Al-Hujurat (The Rooms) 49.12 Revealed in Madinah

يَا أَيُّهَا الَّذِينَ آمَنُوا اجْتَنِبُوا كَثِيرًا مِنَ الظَّنِّ إِنَّ بَعْضَ الظَّنِّ إِثْمٌ وَلَا تَجَسَّسُوا وَلَا يَغْتَبْ بَعْضُكُمْ بَعْضًا (...) ﴿١٢﴾

DAY # 10

I CAN LEARN FROM THE QURAN

Hearsay, making assumptions, and accusing others without evidence is negative, and is to be avoided.

 TO BECOME A BETTER PERSON

Always validating a situation before making a judgement helps me to avoid spreading false information and nurtures my critical thinking.

 WITH THE HELP OF ALLAH

O, Allah! Help me to avoid making assumptions and to always validate the truth.

END WITH AL-HAMDOULLILLAH

🕊 **DAY # 10** 🕊

START WITH BISMILLAH

لَا تَقْنَطُوا مِنْ رَحْمَةِ اللَّهِ

Do not lose hope in Allah's mercy

📖 WHAT THE HOLY QURAN TELLS US ABOUT THIS

(53) Say, 'O Prophet, that Allah says,' "O My servants who have exceeded the limits against their souls! Do not lose hope in Allah's mercy, for Allah certainly forgives all sins. He is indeed the All-Forgiving, Most Merciful.

Az-Zumar (The Troops) 39.53 Revealed in Makkah

قُلْ يَا عِبَادِيَ الَّذِينَ أَسْرَفُوا عَلَىٰ أَنْفُسِهِمْ لَا تَقْنَطُوا مِنْ رَحْمَةِ اللَّهِ إِنَّ اللَّهَ يَغْفِرُ الذُّنُوبَ جَمِيعًا إِنَّهُ هُوَ الْغَفُورُ الرَّحِيمُ ﴿٥٣﴾

DAY # 11

☺ I CAN LEARN FROM THE QURAN

Allah is merciful. As humans, we sometimes make mistakes and wrong choices. If we ask for forgiveness from our heart, we will be forgiven.

☆ TO BECOME A BETTER PERSON

Not losing hope in Allah's mercy nurtures my resilience. Asking for forgiveness keeps me humble.

♡ WITH THE HELP OF ALLAH

O, Allah! Please forgive me for all my wrongdoing.

END WITH AL-HAMDOULLILLAH ☽

 DAY # 11

START WITH BISMILLAH

لَا تَحْزَنْ إِنَّ اللَّهَ مَعَنَا

Do not worry, Allah is with us

📖 WHAT THE HOLY QURAN TELLS US ABOUT THIS

(40) If you do not help him, Allah has already helped him, when those who disbelieved expelled him, and he was the second of two in the cave. He said to his friend, "Do not worry, Allah is with us." (...).

At-Tawbah (The Repentance) 9.40 Revealed in Madinah

إِلَّا تَنْصُرُوهُ فَقَدْ نَصَرَهُ اللَّهُ إِذْ أَخْرَجَهُ الَّذِينَ كَفَرُوا ثَانِيَ اثْنَيْنِ إِذْ هُمَا فِي الْغَارِ إِذْ يَقُولُ لِصَاحِبِهِ لَا تَحْزَنْ إِنَّ اللَّهَ مَعَنَا (...) ﴿٤٠﴾

🕊 DAY # 12 🕊

☺ I CAN LEARN FROM THE QURAN

Whenever we are afraid or feeling lonely, we should remember when our Prophet (PBUH) and Abu Bakar (R.A) were hiding in a cave, away from the ones who were chasing them. They placed their faith in Allah, knowing that He was protecting them.

☆ TO BECOME A BETTER PERSON

Knowing that Allah is always there for me makes me feel safe and reinforces my inner strength. With Him by my side, I know that I can accomplish anything.

♡ WITH THE HELP OF ALLAH

O, Allah! Help me to nurture my faith in you.

END WITH AL-HAMDOULLILLAH ☽

 DAY # 12

START WITH BISMILLAH

إِنَّ الصَّلَاةَ تَنْهَى عَنِ الْفَحْشَاءِ وَالْمُنْكَرِ

Prayer prohibits immorality and wrongdoing

📖 WHAT THE HOLY QURAN TELLS US ABOUT THIS

(45) Recite, [O Muhammad], what has been revealed to you of the Book and establish prayer. Indeed, prayer prohibits immorality and wrongdoing, and the remembrance of Allah is greater. And Allah knows that which you do.

Al-'Ankabut (The Spider) 29.45 Revealed in Makkah

اتْلُ مَا أُوحِيَ إِلَيْكَ مِنَ الْكِتَابِ وَأَقِمِ الصَّلَاةَ ۖ إِنَّ الصَّلَاةَ تَنْهَى عَنِ الْفَحْشَاءِ وَالْمُنْكَرِ ۗ وَلَذِكْرُ اللَّهِ أَكْبَرُ ۗ وَاللَّهُ يَعْلَمُ مَا تَصْنَعُونَ ۝

 **DAY # 13**

☺ I CAN LEARN FROM THE QURAN

When we pray with sincerity and awareness, it purifies our heart. It helps us to focus on the good and avoid making wrong choices or actions. Allah knows when we pray wholeheartedly.

☆ TO BECOME A BETTER PERSON

Praying, with all my heart, helps me to stay on the right path. Doing what is right brings me joy.

♡ WITH THE HELP OF ALLAH

O, Allah! Please give me the strength to do my prayers wholeheartedly so that I can always stay on the right path.

END WITH AL-HAMDOULLILLAH 🌙

 DAY # 13

START WITH BISMILLAH

إِنَّهُ عَلِيمٌ بِذَاتِ الصُّدُورِ

He knows best what is hidden in the heart

📖 WHAT THE HOLY QURAN TELLS US ABOUT THIS

(12) Indeed, those in awe of their Lord without seeing Him- will have forgiveness and a mighty reward. (13) Whether you speak secretly or openly—He surely knows best what is 'hidden' in the heart.

Al-Mulk (The Sovereignty) 67.13 Revealed in Makkah

إِنَّ الَّذِينَ يَخْشَوْنَ رَبَّهُمْ بِالْغَيْبِ لَهُمْ مَغْفِرَةٌ وَأَجْرٌ كَبِيرٌ ۝ وَأَسِرُّوا
قَوْلَكُمْ أَوِ اجْهَرُوا بِهِ ۖ إِنَّهُ عَلِيمٌ بِذَاتِ الصُّدُورِ ۝

 **DAY # 14**

☺ I CAN LEARN FROM THE QURAN

Allah knows all that is within our hearts. Whether we speak out loud, or hold it inside, He knows.

☆ TO BECOME A BETTER PERSON

When I worship Allah, even without seeing Him, follow His commands, and do good deeds without exhibit, I reinforce my faith. He surely knows what I am thinking and sees what I am doing.

♡ WITH THE HELP OF ALLAH

O, Allah! Accept my Duas and remove every impurity from my heart, as you know whatever is inside.

END WITH AL-HAMDOULLILLAH 🌙

 DAY # 14

START WITH BISMILLAH

فَٱصْبِرْ صَبْرًا جَمِيلًا

So endure with beautiful patience

📖 WHAT THE HOLY QURAN TELLS US ABOUT THIS

(5) So endure 'this denial, O Prophet,'

with beautiful patience.

Al-Ma'arij (The Ascending Stairways) 70.5 Revealed in Makkah

فَٱصْبِرْ صَبْرًا جَمِيلًا ۝

 DAY # 15

☺ I CAN LEARN FROM THE QURAN

Beautiful patience means to remain patient through hardships, difficult situations or when experiencing sadness, knowing that Allah is with us. We should remain patient without despair, just like our Prophet (PBUH) was.

☆ TO BECOME A BETTER PERSON

By being patient, I build my perseverance. Practicing patience makes me more patient. It also helps me to make thoughtful decisions.

♡ WITH THE HELP OF ALLAH

O, Allah! Help me to remain patient through any hardship.

END WITH AL-HAMDOULLILLAH ☾

 DAY # 15

START WITH BISMILLAH

قَالَ رَبِّ إِنِّي ظَلَمْتُ نَفْسِي فَاغْفِرْ لِي

My Lord, I have wronged myself, so forgive me

📖 WHAT THE HOLY QURAN TELLS US ABOUT THIS

(16) He said, "My Lord, I have wronged myself, so forgive me." So He forgave him. He is the Forgiver, the Merciful.

Al-Qasas (The Stories) 28.16 Revealed in Makkah

قَالَ رَبِّ إِنِّي ظَلَمْتُ نَفْسِي فَاغْفِرْ لِي فَغَفَرَ لَهُ ۚ إِنَّهُ هُوَ الْغَفُورُ الرَّحِيمُ ﴿١٦﴾

DAY # 16

☺ I CAN LEARN FROM THE QURAN

Whenever we think we may have done wrong, or made an unintentional mistake, we should accept it humbly and ask Allah for forgiveness.

☆ TO BECOME A BETTER PERSON

Asking for forgiveness helps me to build strong relationships with God and with others. It helps my heart rejoice.

♡ WITH THE HELP OF ALLAH

O, Allah! Please help me to ask for forgiveness and to learn from my mistakes.

END WITH AL-HAMDOULLILLAH ☽

 DAY # 16

START WITH BISMILLAH

ادْعُونِي أَسْتَجِبْ لَكُمْ

Call upon Me, I will respond to you

📖 WHAT THE HOLY QURAN TELLS US ABOUT THIS

(60) Your Lord has proclaimed, "Call upon Me, I will respond to you. Surely those who are too proud to worship Me will enter Hell, fully humbled."

Al-Ghafir (The Forgiver) 40.60 Revealed in Makkah

وَقَالَ رَبُّكُمُ ادْعُونِي أَسْتَجِبْ لَكُمْ إِنَّ الَّذِينَ يَسْتَكْبِرُونَ عَنْ عِبَادَتِي سَيَدْخُلُونَ جَهَنَّمَ دَاخِرِينَ ۝

 **DAY # 17**

😊 I CAN LEARN FROM THE QURAN

Whenever we pray wholeheartedly and ask for Allah's help, we should remember that He will always be there for us.

☆ TO BECOME A BETTER PERSON

Asking Allah for help allows me to fortify my connection with Him. It helps me to build my resilience.

♡ WITH THE HELP OF ALLAH

O, Allah! Thank you for listening to my prayers. I am greatful for Your presence.

END WITH AL-HAMDOULLILLAH 🌙

 DAY # 17

START WITH BISMILLAH

وَمَا تَوْفِيقِى إِلَّا بِاللَّهِ

My success lies only with Allah

📖 WHAT THE HOLY QURAN TELLS US ABOUT THIS

(88) He said, "O my people, have you considered? What if I have clear evidence from my Lord, and He has given me good livelihood from Himself? I have no desire to do what I forbid you from doing. I desire nothing but reform, as far as I can. My success lies only with Allah. In Him I trust, and to Him I turn."

Hud (Hud) 11.88 Revealed in Makkah

قَالَ يَا قَوْمِ أَرَأَيْتُمْ إِنْ كُنْتُ عَلَىٰ بَيِّنَةٍ مِنْ رَبِّي وَرَزَقَنِي مِنْهُ رِزْقًا حَسَنًا ۚ وَمَا أُرِيدُ أَنْ أُخَالِفَكُمْ إِلَىٰ مَا أَنْهَاكُمْ عَنْهُ ۚ إِنْ أُرِيدُ إِلَّا الْإِصْلَاحَ مَا اسْتَطَعْتُ ۚ وَمَا تَوْفِيقِي إِلَّا بِاللَّهِ ۚ عَلَيْهِ تَوَكَّلْتُ وَإِلَيْهِ أُنِيبُ ﴿٨٨﴾

DAY # 18

☺ I CAN LEARN FROM THE QURAN

Allah is great. He has given us everything. All of our blessings come from Him. We should place our trust in Him and turn to Him for help and support. For He is always there for us.

☆ TO BECOME A BETTER PERSON

Being grateful for my blessings and knowing that I can always turn to Allah for help, strengthens my faith. Placing my trust in Him helps me to remember that I can achieve anything.

♡ WITH THE HELP OF ALLAH

O, Allah! Remind me of Your presence and to be grateful for my blessings.

END WITH AL-HAMDOULLILLAH 🌙

 DAY # 18

START WITH BISMILLAH

وَقُل رَّبِّ زِدۡنِى عِلۡمًا

My Lord! Increase me in knowledge

WHAT THE HOLY QURAN TELLS US ABOUT THIS

(114) Exalted is Allah, the True King! Do not rush to recite 'a revelation of' the Quran 'O Prophet' before it is 'properly' conveyed to you, and pray, "My Lord! Increase me in knowledge."

Taha (Ta-ha) 20.114 Revealed in Makkah

فَتَعَالَى اللَّهُ الْمَلِكُ الْحَقُّ ۗ وَلَا تَعْجَلْ بِالْقُرْآنِ مِن قَبۡلِ أَن يُقۡضَىٰٓ إِلَيۡكَ وَحۡيُهُۥ ۖ وَقُل رَّبِّ زِدۡنِى عِلۡمًا ﴿١١٤﴾

DAY # 19

☺ I CAN LEARN FROM THE QURAN

This is a beautiful Dua which Allah taught our Prophet Mohammad (PBUH) as he was learning to read the Quran. Whenever we face difficulty in learning something new, we should remember to ask Allah to assist us.

☆ TO BECOME A BETTER PERSON

Keeping on learning helps me to increase my knowledge. Increasing my knowledge keeps my brain active and helps me to become better at problem-solving, communication, and decision-making.

♡ WITH THE HELP OF ALLAH

O, Allah! Help me as I learn so I can improve every day.

END WITH AL-HAMDOULLILLAH ☾

 DAY # 19

START WITH BISMILLAH

وَاللَّهُ خَيْرُ الرَّازِقِينَ

Allah is the Best Provider

WHAT THE HOLY QURAN TELLS US ABOUT THIS

(11) When they saw the fanfare along with the caravan, they 'almost all' flocked to it, leaving you 'O Prophet' standing 'on the pulpit'. Say, "What is with Allah is far better than amusement and merchandise. And Allah is the Best Provider."

Al-Jumu'ah (The Congregation, Friday) 62.11 Revealed in Madinah

وَإِذَا رَأَوْا تِجَارَةً أَوْ لَهْوًا انفَضُّوا إِلَيْهَا وَتَرَكُوكَ قَائِمًا ۚ قُلْ مَا عِندَ اللَّهِ خَيْرٌ مِّنَ اللَّهْوِ وَمِنَ التِّجَارَةِ ۚ وَاللَّهُ خَيْرُ الرَّازِقِينَ ﴿١١﴾

 DAY # 20

😊 I CAN LEARN FROM THE QURAN

Allah reminds us not to forget what is important, and not choose diversion over what is essential (like not neglecting our family). By doing so, Allah will always provide and support all our needs.

⭐ TO BECOME A BETTER PERSON

Not letting myself get distracted by what is unnecessary helps me to build my focus and prioritize what is most important.

♡ WITH THE HELP OF ALLAH

O, Allah! Help me to focus on what is most essential.

END WITH AL-HAMDOULLILLAH 🌙

 DAY # 20

START WITH BISMILLAH

وَيُحِقُّ اللَّهُ الْحَقَّ بِكَلِمَاتِهِ

Allah establishes the truth by His Words

📖 WHAT THE HOLY QURAN TELLS US ABOUT THIS

(80) When the magicians came, Moses said to them, "Cast whatever you wish to cast!" (81) When they did, Moses said, "What you have produced is mere magic, Allah will surely make it useless, for Allah certainly does not set right the work of the corruptors. (82) And Allah establishes the truth by His Words—even to the dismay of the wicked."

Yunus (Jonah) 10.82 Revealed in Makkah

فَلَمَّا جَاءَ السَّحَرَةُ قَالَ لَهُمْ مُوسَىٰ أَلْقُوا مَا أَنْتُمْ مُلْقُونَ ۝ فَلَمَّا أَلْقَوْا قَالَ مُوسَىٰ مَا جِئْتُمْ بِهِ السِّحْرُ ۚ إِنَّ اللَّهَ سَيُبْطِلُهُ ۖ إِنَّ اللَّهَ لَا يُصْلِحُ عَمَلَ الْمُفْسِدِينَ ۝ وَيُحِقُّ اللَّهُ الْحَقَّ بِكَلِمَاتِهِ وَلَوْ كَرِهَ الْمُجْرِمُونَ ۝

DAY # 21

🙂 I CAN LEARN FROM THE QURAN

The truth always prevails, even if some people may not believe it or realize it yet. Allah always shows us the truth.

☆ TO BECOME A BETTER PERSON

Always standing by the truth and following Allah's word helps me to become a trustworthy person. It nurtures my honesty.

♡ WITH THE HELP OF ALLAH

O, Allah! Help me know what is right in every situation.

END WITH AL-HAMDOULLILLAH 🌙

 DAY # 21

START WITH BISMILLAH

إِنْ أَجْرِيَ إِلَّا عَلَى اللَّهِ

My reward is only from Allah

📖 WHAT THE HOLY QURAN TELLS US ABOUT THIS

(72) And if you turn away, 'remember' I have never demanded a reward from you 'for delivering the message'. My reward is only from Allah. And I have been commanded to be one of those who submit 'to Allah'."

Yunus (Jonah) 10.72 Revealed in Makkah

فَإِنْ تَوَلَّيْتُمْ فَمَا سَأَلْتُكُم مِّنْ أَجْرٍ ۖ إِنْ أَجْرِيَ إِلَّا عَلَى اللَّهِ ۖ وَأُمِرْتُ أَنْ أَكُونَ مِنَ الْمُسْلِمِينَ ۝

 **DAY # 22**

☺ I CAN LEARN FROM THE QURAN

When we do good, we should never expect anything in return. Our good deeds are for the sake of Allah. Only He shall reward us for our good deeds.

☆ TO BECOME A BETTER PERSON

Doing good without exhibiting and without expecting anything in return, if only a reward from Allah, helps me to cultivate my generosity.

♡ WITH THE HELP OF ALLAH

O, Allah! May my intentions always be pure. May You reward me for my good deeds.

END WITH AL-HAMDOULLILLAH ☾

 DAY # 22

START WITH BISMILLAH

إِنَّهُ لَا يُحِبُّ الْمُسْتَكْبِرِينَ

He does not like the arrogant

WHAT THE HOLY QURAN TELLS US ABOUT THIS

(22) Your God is 'only' One God. As for those who do not believe in the Hereafter, their hearts are in denial, and they are too proud. (23) Without a doubt, Allah knows what they conceal and what they reveal. He does not like the arrogant.

An-Nahl (The Bee) 16.23 Revealed in Makkah

إِلَهُكُمْ إِلَهٌ وَاحِدٌ ۚ فَالَّذِينَ لَا يُؤْمِنُونَ بِالْآخِرَةِ قُلُوبُهُمْ مُنْكِرَةٌ وَهُمْ مُسْتَكْبِرُونَ ۩ لَا جَرَمَ أَنَّ اللَّهَ يَعْلَمُ مَا يُسِرُّونَ وَمَا يُعْلِنُونَ ۚ إِنَّهُ لَا يُحِبُّ الْمُسْتَكْبِرِينَ ۩

DAY # 23

😊 I CAN LEARN FROM THE QURAN

Believing in our hearts that Allah is our One God keeps us from showing the arrogance that the Almighty dislikes.

⭐ TO BECOME A BETTER PERSON

When I humble myself before Allah and believe wholeheartedly in His promises, I foster my belief and strengthen my self-confidence.

♡ WITH THE HELP OF ALLAH

O, Allah! Keep me humble before You and remove any arrogance from my heart.

END WITH AL-HAMDOULLILLAH

 DAY # 23

START WITH BISMILLAH

وَمَا أَرْسَلْنَاكَ إِلَّا رَحْمَةً لِلْعَالَمِينَ

We did not send you except as mercy to mankind

📖 WHAT THE HOLY QURAN TELLS US ABOUT THIS

(105) We have written in the Psalms, after the Reminder, that the earth will be inherited by My righteous servants. (106) Indeed, in this is a message for people who worship. (107) We did not send you except as mercy to mankind.

Al-Anbya (The Prophets) 21.107 Revealed in Makkah

وَلَقَدْ كَتَبْنَا فِي الزَّبُورِ مِنْ بَعْدِ الذِّكْرِ أَنَّ الْأَرْضَ يَرِثُهَا عِبَادِيَ الصَّالِحُونَ ﴿١٠٥﴾ إِنَّ فِي هَذَا لَبَلَاغًا لِقَوْمٍ عَابِدِينَ ﴿١٠٦﴾ وَمَا أَرْسَلْنَاكَ إِلَّا رَحْمَةً لِلْعَالَمِينَ ﴿١٠٧﴾

DAY # 24

☺ I CAN LEARN FROM THE QURAN

Prophet Muhammad (PBUH) is a role model for humanity. Allah sent us our Prophet to show us mercy. We should follow his footsteps and show compassion to everyone.

☆ TO BECOME A BETTER PERSON

Following Prophet Mohammad's (PBUH) example reinforces my faith. Showing compassion towards others helps me to keep my heart open and understand the feeling of others.

♡ WITH THE HELP OF ALLAH

O, Allah! Help me to follow the steps of our Prophet and to cultivate my compassion.

END WITH AL-HAMDOULLILLAH 🌙

 DAY # 24

START WITH BISMILLAH

وَرَحْمَتِي وَسِعَتْ كُلَّ شَيْءٍ

My mercy encompasses everything

📖 WHAT THE HOLY QURAN TELLS US ABOUT THIS

(156) Ordain for us what is good in this life and the next. Indeed, we have turned to You 'in repentance'." Allah replied, "I will inflict My torment on whoever I will. But My mercy encompasses everything. I will ordain mercy for those who shun evil, pay alms-tax, and believe in Our revelations.

Al-A'raf (The Heights) 7.156 Revealed in Makkah

وَاكْتُبْ لَنَا فِي هَٰذِهِ الدُّنْيَا حَسَنَةً وَفِي الْآخِرَةِ إِنَّا هُدْنَا إِلَيْكَ ۚ قَالَ عَذَابِي أُصِيبُ بِهِ مَنْ أَشَاءُ ۖ وَرَحْمَتِي وَسِعَتْ كُلَّ شَيْءٍ ۚ فَسَأَكْتُبُهَا لِلَّذِينَ يَتَّقُونَ وَيُؤْتُونَ الزَّكَاةَ وَالَّذِينَ هُمْ بِآيَاتِنَا يُؤْمِنُونَ ۝

🕊️ **DAY # 25** 🕊️

☺ I CAN LEARN FROM THE QURAN

Allah is the most merciful, particularly for those who remember Him, who do good deeds, and who follow His words.

☆ TO BECOME A BETTER PERSON

Recognizing Allah's mercy helps me to build my gratitude. Knowing that Allah will have mercy on me, helps me to reinforce my compassion for others.

♡ WITH THE HELP OF ALLAH

O, Allah! Please have mercy on me, on my friends and on my family.

END WITH AL-HAMDOULLILLAH ☾

🕊 DAY # 25 🕊

START WITH BISMILLAH

فَاذْكُرُونِي أَذْكُرْكُمْ

Remember Me; I will remember you

(152) Remember Me; I will remember you. And thank Me, and never be ungrateful.

Al-Baqarah (The Cow) 2.152 Revealed in Madinah

فَاذْكُرُونِي أَذْكُرْكُمْ وَاشْكُرُوا لِي وَلَا تَكْفُرُونِ ۝

 DAY # 26

☺ I CAN LEARN FROM THE QURAN

Allah remembers the ones who think of Him by thanking Him, reciting His name, and praying. Allah loves us and watches over us. We should be grateful for His protection.

☆ TO BECOME A BETTER PERSON

Thinking of Allah and being thankful for His love and for everything that I have, keeps my heart tranquil.

♡ WITH THE HELP OF ALLAH

O, Allah! Help me to always remember You and to follow Your guidance.

END WITH AL-HAMDOULLILLAH 🌙

 DAY # 26

START WITH BISMILLAH

اِنَّ وَعْدَ اللَّهِ حَقٌّ

Allah's promise is true

(5) O humanity! Indeed, Allah's promise is true. So do not let the life of this world deceive you, nor let the Chief Deceiver deceive you about Allah.

Fatir (Originator) 35.5 Revealed in Makkah

يَا أَيُّهَا النَّاسُ إِنَّ وَعْدَ اللَّهِ حَقٌّ فَلَا تَغُرَّنَّكُمُ الْحَيَاةُ الدُّنْيَا وَلَا يَغُرَّنَّكُمْ بِاللَّهِ الْغَرُورُ ۝

DAY # 27

☺ I CAN LEARN FROM THE QURAN

All the promises of Allah are true. One of God's promises is Judgment Day, leading us to the Hereafter. We should remember to do good daily.

☆ TO BECOME A BETTER PERSON

Placing my faith in Allah's promise reinforces my devotion. It reminds me to do good around me daily and makes me feel at peace.

♡ WITH THE HELP OF ALLAH

O, Allah! You are the Greatest! I believe in your promises.

END WITH AL-HAMDOULLILLAH ☾

 DAY # 27

START WITH BISMILLAH

إِنَّ رَبِّي قَرِيبٌ مُجِيبٌ

My Lord is Near and Responsive

📖 WHAT THE HOLY QURAN TELLS US ABOUT THIS

(61) And to Thamood, their brother Saleh. He said, "O my people, worship Allah, you have no god other than Him. He initiated you from the earth, and settled you in it. So seek His forgiveness, and repent to Him. My Lord is Near and Responsive."

Hud (Hud) 11.61 Revealed in Makkah

وَإِلَىٰ ثَمُودَ أَخَاهُمْ صَالِحًا ۚ قَالَ يَا قَوْمِ اعْبُدُوا اللَّهَ مَا لَكُمْ مِنْ إِلَٰهٍ غَيْرُهُ هُوَ أَنْشَأَكُمْ مِنَ الْأَرْضِ وَاسْتَعْمَرَكُمْ فِيهَا فَاسْتَغْفِرُوهُ ثُمَّ تُوبُوا إِلَيْهِ ۚ إِنَّ رَبِّي قَرِيبٌ مُجِيبٌ ﴿٦١﴾

DAY # 28

☺ I CAN LEARN FROM THE QURAN

Allah is near us. He is with us, listens to us, and knows everything about us. Whenever we need Him, we can ask for His help and He will respond.

☆ TO BECOME A BETTER PERSON

Praying and meditating help me nurture my relationship with Allah. It helps me to remain serene and to strengthen my focus.

♡ WITH THE HELP OF ALLAH

O, Allah! I know you are listening to me. Please accept my prayers.

END WITH AL-HAMDOULLILLAH ☽

 DAY # 28

START WITH BISMILLAH

تَوَكَّلْ عَلَى اللَّهِ

Put your trust in Allah

📖 WHAT THE HOLY QURAN TELLS US ABOUT THIS

(1) O Prophet! Fear Allah, and do not obey the unbelievers and the hypocrites. Allah is Knowledgeable and Wise. (2) And follow what is revealed to you from your Lord. Allah is fully aware of what you do. (3) And put your trust in Allah. Allah is enough as a trustee.

Al-Ahzab (The Combined Forces) 33.3 Revealed in Madinah

يَا أَيُّهَا النَّبِيُّ اتَّقِ اللَّهَ وَلَا تُطِعِ الْكَافِرِينَ وَالْمُنَافِقِينَ ۗ إِنَّ اللَّهَ كَانَ عَلِيمًا حَكِيمًا ۞ وَاتَّبِعْ مَا يُوحَى إِلَيْكَ مِنْ رَبِّكَ ۚ إِنَّ اللَّهَ كَانَ بِمَا تَعْمَلُونَ خَبِيرًا ۞ وَتَوَكَّلْ عَلَى اللَّهِ ۚ وَكَفَى بِاللَّهِ وَكِيلًا ۞

🕊 DAY # 29 🕊

☺ I CAN LEARN FROM THE QURAN

We should not worry about what others think or believe about us. We should place our faith in Allah, and know that He has the power to help us when we are in need. He is all that we need.

☆ TO BECOME A BETTER PERSON

Placing my faith in Allah and not worrying about what others may think helps me to focus on my own growth. It builds my self-confidence.

♡ WITH THE HELP OF ALLAH

O, Allah! Help me to mute unnecessary opinions, and to reinforce my faith in You.

END WITH AL-HAMDOULLILLAH ☾

 DAY # 29

START WITH BISMILLAH

هُوَ مَعَكُمْ أَيْنَ مَا كُنْتُمْ

He is with you wherever you are

📖 WHAT THE HOLY QURAN TELLS US ABOUT THIS

(4) He is the One Who created the heavens and the earth in six Days, then established Himself on the Throne. He knows whatever goes into the earth and whatever comes out of it, and whatever descends from the sky and whatever ascends into it. And He is with you wherever you are. For Allah is All-Seeing of what you do.

Al-Hadid (The Iron) 57.4 Revealed in Madinah

هُوَ الَّذِى خَلَقَ السَّمَاوَاتِ وَالْأَرْضَ فِى سِتَّةِ أَيَّامٍ ثُمَّ اسْتَوَىٰ عَلَى الْعَرْشِ يَعْلَمُ مَا يَلِجُ فِى الْأَرْضِ وَمَا يَخْرُجُ مِنْهَا وَمَا يَنْزِلُ مِنَ السَّمَاءِ وَمَا يَعْرُجُ فِيهَا ۖ وَهُوَ مَعَكُمْ أَيْنَ مَا كُنْتُمْ ۚ وَاللَّهُ بِمَا تَعْمَلُونَ بَصِيرٌ ۝

DAY # 30

😊 I CAN LEARN FROM THE QURAN

Allah knows everything, He is everywhere and His power encompasses everything. He is with us wherever we are, and is always watching over us.

☆ TO BECOME A BETTER PERSON

Knowing that Allah is with me makes me feel strong. It nurtures my fortitude.

♡ WITH THE HELP OF ALLAH

O, Allah! I know that you are always watching over me. Thank You for Your presence.

END WITH AL-HAMDOULLILLAH 🌙

 DAY # 30

We sincerely hope that you enjoyed this book.
We worked diligently to bring to light the essential values
of Islam to help our children fulfill their highest potential.

If you believe we can further enhance our content, please
don't hesitate to contact us at :

info@goodheartedbooks.com

Otherwise, feel free to rate and share your review.

Thank you!

Made in the USA
Monee, IL
08 April 2023